MW00596523

Dogs have Masters,

Cats have Staff

A Great Cat Training Guide dealing with Cat Spraying, Cat Bed, Cat Litter, Clicker Training, etc.

By Butch Spillman

Description

If you are a cat owner who has become stressed over certain behaviors your cat exhibits, you are not alone. Cats have their own way of doing things and their natural instincts kick in on a regular basis. Although it might be natural for them, it can be annoying for us.

With this easy-to-understand guide, you will find it simple to train your cat and curb those behaviors you do not enjoy. From litter box training to keeping your cat off your counters, you will find useful information and techniques to help you make your cat a more enjoyable member of your family.

My hope is that you are happy with your new Cat Training book. If you can, please leave an honest review.

TABLE OF CONTENTS

All Rights Reserved.
No part of this publication may be reproduced in any form or by any means, including scanning, photocopying, or otherwise without prior written permission of the copyright holder.

Paul "Butch" Spillman
Copyright © 2018

Introduction

Training a cat can be a daunting experience, especially if the cat has developed many bad habits over the years. Although working with a kitten makes training easier, it is possible to train an older cat but it will take more patience.

To prove cats can be trained, I invite you to conduct a little experiment. You will be shocked to see your cat trained in only seven days. Although this is not a part of the full cat training this book offers, it is simply a means for you to realize it is possible to train that furry friend of yours and get him to start seeing things your way (at least the majority of the time).

For the next seven days, plan on feeding your cat at the exact same time every single day. It is important you do this at the same exact time each day so your cat will begin to develop a habit of being fed at that time. Even though your cat doesn't own a watch, he will quickly learn what time of the day he will be fed.

On the eighth day, do not feed him at the normal time and you are sure to find him becoming upset and letting you have it with his barrage of "meows" and flicks of his tail. Your cat will verbally demand you feed him at the time he has grown accustomed to being fed at. He will be there to remind you and make sure you never forget again.

It is amazing to see this happen because it proves cats can be trained. In a week's time, you will have trained your cat to know when to expect to be fed. This little exercise often encourages doubtful cat owners who think there is no way their feline friend will be able to be trained.

It is important cat owners realize even the most stubborn of cats can be trained when using the right methods. A cat cannot be trained to perform certain tasks like a dog can because they have a mind that is constantly calculating.

For instance, Fluffy is not going to be trained to sit or stay like his dog friends can but there are certain "tricks" cats can be trained to do. Although a dog will perform a trick because it makes his owner happy, cats need further motivation.

Neither a dog nor a cat can understand English (though we wish they could). These animals understand the tone of our voice and certain hand gestures we make during the training process. Before you can begin training your cat or kitten, you need to learn what gets their attention and use that angle to get them to pay attention during the training process.

When training a dog, treats are used to entice the dog to do the trick. Once the cat trick has been learned and the dog sees it pleases his owner, he will continue to perform the trick, even if he is not rewarded with a treat.

This is entirely the opposite of what can be experienced with a cat. If you want a cat to do something, you are going to have to offer a treat each and every time. Without the incentive of a treat, the cat will likely refuse to do your bidding, even if you ask in the sweetest of tones.

The most important thing you will need to remember as a cat owner is this: Your dog will want to please you but your cat will expect you to please him.

Cats will only do tricks if they get something out of it that pleases them. Anyone who has ever owned a cat should understand cats are only motivated by things that bring them pleasure. They could care less about pleasing you. Sorry if that bursts your bubble!

If you want to get the very best results with training, it is best to start with a kitten. Kittens are still too small to have developed a snotty attitude so they will be easier to train. It is best to start as young as possible but the training should not begin until an owner has had a kitten for a couple of weeks.

Kittens are easier to train because they are more curious at this time and will crave attention from you. Because they have not yet developed any bad habits, they will be easier to mold into calm and obedient cats.

In a sense, you will not be training your cat or kitten. Instead, you are exposing them to the good habits and behaviors you want them to develop. Hopefully, they will choose to adopt these good habits and behaviors with as little resistance as possible.

As you continue to read, you will better understand your cat and how his mind works. You will know what goes on in the mind of a cat and you will learn proven strategies that will help you litter box train him, teach him how to be social with other humans, and how to even perform certain tricks.

Once you have learned the basics of cat training, you will feel more confident to take this training and use it to completely mold your cat into a more loveable and obedient creature, though he will never entirely lose his "superior to though" attitude and we true cat lovers wouldn't have it any other way.

Before you get started with cat training, it is important to read through the entire guide so you will have a full understanding of the journey you are about to embark on. Although it won't be easy, the end result will leave you and your cat with an unbreakable bond.

You are about to delve into the world of what makes cats tick and how their minds work. When you learn this information, you will be able to discover the right techniques to use on your cat so he ends up thinking his newfound training was his own idea.

Cat training is something that no owner should fear. It does not require you to purchase any fancy equipment or attend long and expensive training classes. You simply need to learn a few facts and techniques to make the job of training your cat as easy as possible.

So, let's get started on your journey towards training that furry friend of yours. You will be amazed at the progress he begins to make as you start on the journey towards his instruction. It won't take long, but it will take effort so be prepared to provide consistent instruction throughout the process.

CHAPTER ONE
Understanding Your Cat's Natural Instincts

Understanding your cat's natural instincts is important before you launch out into training. If you do not understand how a cat naturally acts and the reasons behind his actions, you are going to likely see them as bad behavior.

It is important to realize your cat is not going to go against his natural instincts to please you. It's just not going to happen and if you are expecting it to, you are in for a rude awakening and a lot of disappointment.

Before we get started on training your cat, let's take a look at some of his natural instincts that may prove problematic for you. The following are the instincts your cat was born with and no matter how you try to change him, he will not.

Chewing – Cats chew for a couple of different reasons. Chewing helps to keep their teeth sharp and clean while massaging their gums for good oral health. Cats also chew on items when they are trying to gain access to them.

Making sounds – Over the life of owning a cat, you will quickly learn he will emit many more sounds than a simple meow. He has a language of his very own and unfortunately, we as humans cannot really understand it. Sometimes, the noises a cat makes can be a bit annoying, especially when the cat seems to go on and on and you can't figure out what he is trying to tell you. It is up to you to learn to decipher his language and this takes time and patience.

Scratching – Cats scratch for many reasons. They scratch in self-defense to protect themselves against harm. They scratch to keep their nails groomed and sharp. They also scratch as a means of marking their territory. If your cat is scratching himself, this could be a sign of fleas or ear mites.

Digging – Most cat owners are shocked to learn their cat likes to dig. If allowed outside, the cat will dig in the dirt just like a dog would. They will also sometimes "dig" in your carpet. This does not necessarily mean the cat is trying to dig a hole so he can use the bathroom. It may simply mean he smells something and wants to investigate to find out what it is.

Spraying – Spraying is something male cats do to mark their territory and it is one of the most annoying natural cat instincts for owners to deal with. If a male cat is continuously spraying, the only effective solution is to have him neutered. This operation will typically stop the problem and aggravation.

Biting – Biting is a means for a cat to protect himself when he feels he is in danger. It is important cat owners protect their cats from feeling as if they are in dangerous situations. It is also important not to play rough with kittens or they can develop the bad habit of biting during play.

Climbing – Cats do not necessarily love to climb but they do like being high above others because it gives them a unique vantage point where they are able to look down on everything and everyone below them. This can be a problem when the cat starts climbing your expensive drapes.

Hiding – Sometimes, it can seem as if cats are anti-social but they really are not, for the most part. Cats typically like dark, small spaces they can hide in. If this bothers you, the only solution is making sure they do not have access to areas they can hide in.

Spilling water – Although many people think cats hate water, this is not entirely true. Cats do not like getting wet but they are quite fascinated with water. This is one of the reasons cats will knock their water bowls over or hang out by the sink and watch the faucet drip. Some cats have even discovered how to flush the toilet just so they can watch the water move.

Pouncing – Pouncing is as natural for a cat is walking is for a human. Although it is a natural instinct, it can be quite painful when a cat pounces on you. To prevent this instinct from making you a victim, make sure to avoid rough play while your cat is a kitten and offer him toys he can pounce on so he will not be so inclined to pounce on you.

Now that you better understand your cat's natural habits, they should not come across to you as being bad behavior. As you will learn in this training book, it is important you offer ways for your cat to act on his natural instincts rather than trying to stop them completely. In the end, cats are going to be cats. If you want them living in your world, you are going to have to provide the right environment and opportunities for them to express these innate inclinations.

CHAPTER TWO
Understanding the Mind of Your Cat

Before even starting on the path to training your cat, you need to understand him. You might think you know him but you might not fully understand how his little mind operates. Knowing how a cat thinks and what his natural inclinations are will be of tremendous help when attempting to train. Without this knowledge, you will likely find yourself being unsuccessful in your efforts.

With this chapter, you will discover how cats think, how they learn, and how they associate things. By the end of this chapter, you will feel better equipped to be able to launch into understanding how to train your cat and feeling confident while doing so.

One of the first things you will quickly discover when attempting to train your cat, is cats do not have long attention spans. While you may be able to spend long periods of time working with and training your dog, cats simply will not put up with this. They lose interest too quickly and will begin grooming themselves or looking for a place to take a nap before you even finish the first demonstration.

While a dog learns best with repetition, a cat learns better with association. When a cat does something and they get a positive response, they will remember it and attempt to do it again.

If the cat gets a negative response from the action they just committed, they will also remember it and avoid doing that action in the future. It is important to note, the response does not have to come from the owner and could simply be the result of the action they just performed.

~Are cats really domesticated?~

Scientists have discovered even though cats have supposedly been domesticated for over 9,000 years, they really are not domesticated at all. They still hold the same instincts they would have out in the wild and have changed very little over the years.

By bringing cats into our homes, we are not providing them with the natural environment they would be in if they were in the wild. They realize this and are doing their very best to navigate this strange land.

To a cat, our drapes look like the perfect places to climb for gaining strength. The corners of our furniture provide them with ideal spots for scratching so they can groom their nails. Kitchen counters appear to be the perfect place to sit and observe the world down below.

Unfortunately, a cat does not understand our environment like we do. As cat owners, we cannot block our cats from expressing their natural instincts. Trying to do so simply will not work. It will lead to frustration for both you and your cat.

When you tell Fluffy, "Stop doing that," Fluffy is not going to understand why you are objecting to them doing something they find natural to do. It is your job as a cat owner to be able to provide them with a better alternative so they can express their natural instincts safely and without causing you aggravation.

~Cats have the memory of an elephant~

It is important to understand a cat's memory is far greater than a dog's. According to scientists, a cat's memory is around 200 times better than that of a dog. Let that sink in for a minute. With such a bountiful ability to remember, it would seem cats would be very easy to train.

To understand why they are not, we need to realize an important fact. Although a cat's memory is much more advanced than that of a dog, they only remember those things they consider important to them and their survival. The rest of the information a cat receives gets filed in the back recesses of their brain, in a dusty file called "Useless."

Cats are very observant animals which is why you will often see them staring at you or staring into what seems like space. They are constantly monitoring the world around them and gauging reactions so they will know how to proceed with action.

When attempting to train a cat, an owner needs to make sure they set up situations that create positive results. A cat will never learn through discipline because it simply does not create a memory in their brain.

As cats observe, they begin to imitate what they discover. Cats are constantly learning and as they experience positive and negative outcomes from their actions, they make necessary changes to their behavior.

Through countless hours of research, scientists have discovered cats are able to retain information that is new to them for about sixteen hours. If an owner is attempting to teach their cat a new trick, they will need to make sure they keep this in mind and repeat the training exercises every sixteen hours so the cat is able to retain this newly learned skill in their memory bank so it is not forgotten. The more the cat does the trick and gets a positive outcome, the better able he will be to remember to perform the trick when offered a treat.

~Discipline does not work for cats~

If you have been attempting to discipline your cat to train him, you are going about things in the wrong way. This is why so many cat owners feel like pulling their hair out when trying to train their cats. This method of training never works so throw it out with your old thinking and learn the right way to engage your cat's interest so he will stop doing the wrong things and learn to do those things that please you.

Like most pets that have been domesticated, cats are more likely to respond to training when they are placed on a set schedule. Constant changes in routine disrupt a cat's thinking and leave them feeling ornery. When a cat has a set schedule of sleep, eat, and play time, they will feel more secure and will be more loving and responsive to their owner. This opens up the training possibilities and helps to prevent needless aggravation.

~Set up a schedule and stick to it~

When you bring your new kitten home, it is imperative you set up a schedule and stick to it from day one. Cats do not like change and even the slightest of schedule changes can cause problems with their behavior and make it seem like they are purposely exhibiting bad behavior when they are really just upset and trying to make sense of the changes in their life.

Once the schedule has been set, it should be followed when at all possible. When changes need to be made, of any type, it is important they are introduced gradually so the cat does not become distressed over the changes and doesn't "act out" to show his dismay over the situation.

~Your cat doesn't know he is being naughty~

One of the biggest mistakes cat owners make is treating their cat on the same level they would a child. Although you see your cat's behavior as being naughty, to your cat it is just natural. He isn't trying to ruin your day, he is just being a cat.

He does not have a concept of naughty or nice and is only doing what comes naturally to him. Once you realize this, you will find yourself much less offended when he decides to pee in your favorite pair of shoes.

It is important cat owners realize their cat is not a fur-covered human. He thinks and acts very differently than you or I would. This is why discipline never works with cats because they simply do not know what discipline is or even why it is being given.

~Your cat thinks he owns you~

Your cat recognizes you as the ruler of the home because you have left your scent everywhere and he has challenged you as the ruler. Each time he rubs his face against you or items in the home, he is marking them as his own.

Cats mark their territory to ensure everyone knows it belongs to them. They will place their scent over your own scent as a means of challenging you like they would other cats in the wild. Because you are bigger than him, he realizes you are dominant but that will not stop him from claiming everything in the house as his.

Although cats view their owners as dominant over them, this does not mean the cat will be obedient. In fact, the cat simply thinks he is peacefully sharing the space equally with you.

~Research reveals what makes cats tick~

Countless hours of research have been put into figuring out cats and how they think. Research has proven simply watching a cat walking around or even doing nothing helps to keep a person's blood pressure down. Cats have a calming effect on humans so it seems we owe them more than we realize.

Reading this book will help you to learn more about your cat so you can live peacefully with him. Not only will your newfound knowledge help you understand how your cat thinks and reacts to the world around him, it will also help you to save your furniture and drapes from being damaged.

Again, it is important to realize cats need a way to express their natural instincts. They would much prefer to use a litter box over going on your carpet, just like they would prefer to use a scratching post over your furniture, as long as the scratching post is made an attractive option to them. In the following chapter, we will discuss simple ways to litter box train your cat. With these cat training techniques, you will be able to have your cat fully trained in one week or less, without pulling your hair out in the process.

CHAPTER THREE
Litter Box Train Your Kitten without Stress

One of the biggest sources of stress for a new kitten owner is kitten litter box training. Just like a parent stresses over potty training their toddler, kitten owners often find the process of litter box training to be arduous.

Litter box training is one of the first things a kitten owner will want to tackle. While some owners are lucky and they receive their new kitten already properly trained, this is not always the case. Luckily, there are some tips that will make training much easier for owners, even if they have never attempted to train a kitten before.

Before you attempt the process of litter box training your kitten, there are a few supplies you will need to purchase. Thankfully, these are fairly inexpensive so you will not need to invest a lot of money into training.

~Purchasing your supplies~

You will need to purchase a litter box for your kitten but it is important to choose one that fits. When just starting out, a smaller box will be needed. When you go to the pet supply shop, you are likely to find a ton of choices available. There are fancy models, covered models, and even expensive models that clean themselves.

Unless you are keen on spending lots of your money, all you really need is a simple plastic box that will hold your kitten and his litter. There is really no need for any fancy litter box, especially in the beginning when your kitten is first learning how to go in the box. A smaller box will be easier for the little guy to climb into so he will be more likely to use the box without issue.

You will also need to purchase litter. This is another area that can be overwhelming for new kitten owners because there are so many types. Just like with the litter box, keeping things simple, especially in the beginning, is important.

Word of caution: Do not use clumping cat litter or any litter that contains silica. Kittens will sometimes lick their paws and accidentally ingest the litter or even eat some it out of the litter box. This type of litter can cause gastrointestinal upset and even blockages so it should be avoided until the kitten is older.

In the beginning, plain clay litter is your best option. Avoid purchasing scented litters which can cause confusion for your kitten. Because of the scent, they will not be able to smell their own pee and poop which is important when they are first learning to go in the box. Plain clay litter is incredibly cheap and can be purchased in twenty-five-pound bags for a few dollars at most retailers.

You will also need to purchase a pooper scooper so you can keep your little guy's litter box nice and clean. These can be purchased for a dollar or less and they come in handy as training continues.

While certainly not a requirement, you may want to purchase litter box liners to make cleanup easier. Some kittens become annoyed over liners and will stop using the litter box. If this happens, discontinue using them.

~It is time to start training~

Now, you have all the litter box training supplies you need for getting started. With the following information, you should be able to easily have your kitten trained in about a week. Some kittens train very quickly while others need a little encouragement. The important thing is to approach the training process when you have plenty of time so you will not find yourself feeling annoyed because you lack time and patience.

First, you will need to find a place where your kitten can be safely placed for about seven to ten days. If you do not have a small enclosed space, you can create one using a baby gate or a large dog crate. Just make sure there is enough room for the kitten to freely roam and room for the litter box, food, and water bowls.

The litter box should only be about 1/3 full of litter. Making it too full will only lead to a mess as your little guy learns to scratch to cover his poop and pee. Too much litter is a waste because it will likely end up all over your floor.

Your kitten needs to grow accustomed to this strange new place. Gently place him inside the litter box and take one of his paws and make a scratching motion in the clean litter. He may find this enjoyable and will start digging in the litter. This is completely normal and he should not be stopped.

In the beginning, your kitten is going to want to play in his litter box and you may even find him sleeping in it. Allow him to do whatever he needs to do so he does not feel threatened by this box.

~Accidents are bound to happen in the beginning~

When you first start litter box training your kitten, you will need to prepare for accidents. If he pees outside of the box, simply take a clean paper towel and blot up the moisture and then rub the pee into his litter so the scent will be there.

Should he poop outside of the box, scoop up the poop and make sure he sees you place it in his litter box. After rubbing the pee into the litter or placing the poop in the litter box, place your kitten inside the box and help him move his paws to cover the poop or pee.

You may have to do this for a few days before he realizes what he needs to do. Later, you will scoop the poop out and clean the litter on a daily basis but do not do this when he is first training. He needs the smell of his poop and pee to be able to know this is his marked spot for using the bathroom.

When accidents occur outside of the litter box, make sure you carefully clean these areas with a pet enzymatic cleaner so the smell will be completely removed and the kitten will not become confused and continue to use the bathroom in these areas.

It is wise to keep the kitten contained in this small area for the full time of training. Even after the kitten seems to understand where to go each time, he needs to be kept in a small area until he is a little older. You must realize his bladder is still very tiny and he will not be able to hold it like an older cat can.

He might find it difficult to make it all the way to his litter box if he is allowed to freely roam throughout your home. Once he has developed bad habits of peeing throughout the house, it can be difficult to break them so it is important to be diligent now, when training will be much easier to accomplish.

~Who is running the show?~

As you are litter box training your kitten, you are going to learn something quite remarkable about him. When a cat covers his poop or pee, he is doing so out of respect for you because he considers you dominant over him.

Cats that consider themselves dominant want other cats and animals to be able to smell their poop and pee so they will refuse to cover it. If you see your kitten use the bathroom in his litter box without covering it, you will know he has not yet realized he is not the king of the castle. This means you might need to work a little harder with him to ensure he knows his place in the home.

~Litter box cleanliness is important~

Keeping your kitten's litter box clean is important. In the beginning, you will need to make sure you allow some poop to stay in the box for a couple of days. Once your kitten has learned the art of pooping and peeing in the box each time they go, you will need to make sure you are careful to keep his litter box clean or you might find unwelcome surprises.

Many cat owners make the mistake of thinking a cat needs some type of clay or sandy material to go on. In reality, if his litter box contains too much poop and he begins to feel uncomfortable, he will go in your laundry basket, on your bed, and anywhere else he can relieve himself. In a pinch, he will even pee or poop on the floor but this is uncommon. Most of the time, cats will try to find a place to go where they can cover their poop or pee.

Now that your cat has mastered his litter box and you feel confident he knows how to go, you can one day consider toilet training him but we will save that topic for an entirely different chapter because it isn't for every owner.

CHAPTER FOUR
Should You Attempt to Toilet Train Your Cat?

You have likely seen videos or pictures of cats doing their business on a human toilet and wondered how someone possibly trained their cat in that manner. Although it almost seems comical, there are some actual benefits to training your cat to use your toilet.

When your cat is toilet trained, you can say goodbye to litter forever and you will never have to worry about scooping poop, dumping the litter, or cleaning up the messes your cat makes with his litter again. For many cat owners, these benefits are well worth the time it takes to introduce your pet to cat toilet training.

This type of training is not for every cat owner so if it makes you feel weird to share your toilet with your furry friend, then you might want to stick to the traditional means of litter box training.

~Is your cat ready for toilet training~

Before you even consider toilet training your cat, you also need to consider your cat and how he will feel about it. Every cat is not a good candidate for this type of training. Some cats find toilets to be a source of fear and older cats may find it difficult to jump up on the toilet due to joint pain. If a cat is already having trouble with their litter box elimination, it is not wise to try and introduce this more complicated means of training them to go in the toilet.

A cat needs to be at least three months of age before toilet training begins. A cat who is not timid is the best candidate though timid cats can also be toilet trained with extra work and patience. There are several steps involved in this training process so make sure you fully understand each one before beginning the training.

- The first step you will need to take is to make sure you decide on the bathroom you want your cat to use. The bathroom should be one that offers easy access and is always available to your cat.
- Once you have decided on the bathroom, you will need to first move your cat's litter box in that

bathroom and give him time to get used to eliminating in the room. This is not a step that should be rushed because it can be confusing for a cat when you suddenly move their litter box to a new location. Make sure you move the litter box closer to the toilet each day until it is resting right next to the toilet. Allow your cat one to two weeks before moving on to the next step in the training process.

- Once the cat is accustomed to his litter box being next to the toilet, you will need to gradually raise the litter box off the ground by about three inches at a time. You will need to do this every other day until the litter box is the same height as your toilet.

- For the next step, you will leave the toilet closed and place the litter box on top of the toilet. Leave the litter box on the toilet lid for a few days, allowing your cat time to grow accustomed to using his litter box in this strange new position. This may take time and patience but do not give up because you will eventually be rewarded with his ability to follow your wishes. Each time he successfully uses the litter box while on top of the toilet, make sure to reward him.

- The next step in toilet training involves the use of trays. If you are using a cat toilet training kit, you will follow the directions for that kit, using the trays in the order recommended.

There are a few different cat toilet training kits on the market and they can make the process of toilet training a cat much easier. Unfortunately, these can sometimes be a little expensive but it is possible to simply make your own. The first tray used features no hole in the middle. It is simply filled with litter and the cat grows accustomed to going on the pan.

As the cat progresses in training, an opening is introduced in the middle of the tray. The hole will be made larger and larger until, eventually, the cat is simply going in the toilet without any litter tray in place.

Word of caution: When using this training method, you will need to make sure you purchase a litter that is safe for flushing. Traditional clay litters can cause severe clogs in a toilet and should never be flushed or even used in this toilet training method.

Although cat owners would relish the thought of getting rid of their kitty litter nightmares, there are some downsides to toilet training a cat. Some veterinarians do not recommend this type of training because cats are not able to eliminate as they naturally would by covering up their waste. For some cats, this can become stressful.

If at any time during the training process your cat seems to become stressed or begins regressing back to eliminating on the floor, it is important for you to carefully evaluate whether or not he is ready to advance in training. Some cats seem just fine with this type of toilet training and others completely refuse to do it. You will simply have to work with your cat to see if this is something he is willing to learn or not.

Although toilet training can be a wonderful thing for owners, you will have to weigh the benefits for you versus the problems it might cause with your cat. In the end, it may not be worth the hassle but you may want to try it if litter has become a true annoyance to you and you would like to say goodbye to it forever.

It is important to note, toilet training should only be attempted in homes where there is only one cat. If you attempt to toilet train more than one cat, you could run into a problem if they all need to go at once.

It is also important to keep enzymatic and anti-bacterial cleaning supplies on hand throughout the training process and even beyond so accidents can be cleaned up quickly and efficiently.

The key to success with toilet training your cat is to be patient with him and the process. If it becomes overwhelming, stop the training and attempt it at another time when your cat is more open to the idea.

CHAPTER FIVE
Stop the Biting and Clawing For No More Pain

There are two weapons a cat can use against you - their claws and teeth. Anyone who has ever been viciously attacked by a scared cat knows this to be true. Cats have extremely sharp teeth and claws which can inflict a great amount of damage and pain very quickly.

~Don't consider declawing~

Of course, you can't remove your cat's teeth because he needs them for eating. Most all veterinarians have stopped the practice of removing the claws because they consider this to be inhumane due to the fact it causes great pain for the cat. It also leaves them basically defenseless, should they ever be let loose into the wild and left to fend for themselves. If you are wondering should I declaw my cat, please don't consider it.

Declawing is considered inhumane because it doesn't just consist of the removal of the claw. The vet will partially amputate each of the cat's digits, up to the knuckle area. Not only is the surgery extremely painful, complications can also arise. Declawing changes the way a cat is able to walk and balance and it should never be considered.

Because neither of these defenses can be removed from the cat, training is in order. Your cat needs to learn when it is suitable for him to use his claws or teeth and when it is not. Like every training step for cats, this step involves association.

Unfortunately, most cat owners go about this training in the wrong way and their efforts to curb the biting and scratching fail. If your cat is scratching and biting you, your furniture, and other people, make sure you read further so you can stop this unwanted behavior in its tracks.

~Ditch the water spray bottle~

One of the first "tricks" cat owners do when they are trying to stop their cat from scratching or biting is to grab a spray bottle and spray their cat with water. There is a big problem with this technique because it does not offer the right level of association.

When the cat gets sprayed in the face with water, he certainly doesn't like it. Unfortunately, he is smart enough to know the spray came from you and not from the furniture or another item he was scratching or biting. Cat spray bottle training simply is not effective.

So, instead of associating the water spray with the bad behavior, he associates it with you. This will only make him wary of you instead of helping to train him to stop the bad behavior.

For the spray bottle trick to work, your cat would have to believe the water spray came from the furniture or another item the cat was scratching on. Unless you have the ability to rig this to happen in some way, your attempts at spraying your cat are useless and will end up causing more harm than good. You want your cat to trust you, not be afraid of you. If you have been using a water bottle on your cat, throw it away now and keep reading.

~Reasons cats want to scratch~

Before we delve further into training techniques, you need to understand why your cat has the natural inclination to scratch. Knowing this will help you to better understand his behaviors and what you can do to make it stop.

- Cats scratch because they are marking their territory. A cat's paws contain scent glands that release his scent when he scratches. Even if he is the only cat in the house, he will feel the need to do this.
- Cats also scratch to keep their nails properly maintained. Cats scratch to remove the outside nail husk that is shed periodically. This action helps to keep their claws healthy and strong.
- Some cats scratch just because it feels good to them. Scratching is a way for a cat to distress and can help them avoid developing other unwanted behaviors.

- When a cat scratches, they are also stretching. The act of scratching stretches their muscles and tendons in their toes, legs, neck, and shoulders. Just like humans have the tendency to stretch when their muscles feel tense, cats will do the same.

Now that you know why your cat likes to scratch your furniture and other items in your home, what can be done to stop it? If your new leather couch is to survive, you will need to be prepared to go through seven days of training with your cat. Are you ready? Let's get started!

~Seven days to no more scratching~

If you will commit to the steps involved for each day, you will easily and effectively be able to train your cat to stop using your furniture and legs as a scratching post. If you follow these steps precisely, you will find this process to be simple and even fun. You may want to print this page to hang on your fridge so you will know what step to take on each of the seven days.

DAY ONE – Purchase a few different scratching posts, depending on the size of your home. You can find cat scratching posts for sale online and in your favorite pet store. If you live in a large home you may need three to four and a small apartment may only require two. When purchasing a scratching post make sure it is large enough and solid so your cat will be able to scratch easily.

DAY TWO – Make sure you place the best scratching posts in the right areas, far from your furniture. The idea is to offer an alternative to your furniture and you do not want to confuse your cat. Ideas for placement include: near a window, near his sleeping area, or in the center of the room.

DAY THREE – It is time to make your couch and other furniture unattractive to your feline friend. You can do this in several different ways, depending on your preferences and what seems to work best for your cat. You can cover the couch with a fitted sheet, carefully tucking it under the legs. You can also cover the couch with aluminum foil as cats hate it. Depending on the material of your couch, you may find double-sided tape provides a deterrent to scratching. Because cats dislike strong citrus odors, spraying a natural orange essence spray on your couch can make it an unwelcome place for your cat.

DAY FOUR – You have most likely heard how much cats love catnip and the rumors are true. You can buy catnip in pet supply stores or herbal markets. Spray the catnip oil all over the cat scratching posts. You can also use honeysuckle or grass as an attractant for your cat.

DAY FIVE – It is time to begin working with your cat on using the scratching posts. One way to get them to discover the posts for themselves is to use a wand toy. Simply begin playing with the cat while using the wand and lead them up the cat scratch post by using the toy. When they reach up to grab the toy, they will realize the material is great for scratching. You can also (if they cooperate) lift them up and gently move their paws over the post, helping them to feel the material and get a whiff of the catnip scent.

DAY SIX – Continue working with your cat using play and positive association. Each time your cat scratches on the post, make sure you reward them with a special treat. Your cat will soon associate treats with scratching on the post and will enjoy the texture of the scratching post so much, they will want to do it even if they are not given a treat. This is one of the times treats do not have to be consistent because the cat will associate pleasure with the post because it will captivate his sense of smell and feel as he enjoys the texture of the post and the smell of the catnip.

DAY SEVEN – By now, your cat should be much more interested in the scratching posts than your furniture. Continue to have fun playing and offering treats when he uses the post. Some cats continue to need further encouragement so do not give up if your cat is not properly trained in seven days.

If you have worked with your cat for a couple of weeks and he still scratches the furniture, you may want to consider nail covers. These are completely harmless and are made of silicone. They are glued over your cat's nails, preventing them from scratching. This should only be used as a last resort. Even though they are completely safe for the cat and your furniture, they do prevent your cat from enjoying the action of scratching.

~Stop your cat from biting or scratching you~

When a cat feels threatened, their natural instinct is to bite or scratch so they can get away to safety. Sometimes, cats bite or scratch because they are being playful and do not realize they are causing pain.

One of the best ways to get a cat to stop biting you or scratching is to realize how cats play with one another. Have you ever seen a couple of kittens "play fighting" with one another? If you have, you have likely seen one bite the other and the victim lets out a loud meow. This meow lets the other cat know he has been hurt so it doesn't happen again.

You can use this same principle to curb your cat's propensity for biting and scratching you. If he scratches or bites you, make sure you let out a very loud "meow" right away. This will scare your cat and he will likely run for cover but it will give him the message that he has hurt you and he will be less likely to do it again in the future. Each time he does this, make sure you verbally let him know. It might feel a little embarrassing at first but once you see how well it works, you won't mind at all.

~What you take away, you must replace~

It is important to remember, each time you take away something from your cat, you need to provide an alternative or else you are not providing the right environment to allow your cat to express his natural inclinations. If you take away the furniture as a scratching post, you must provide a scratching post. If you don't want him sleeping on your favorite chair, you must provide a comfy sleeping area of his own. Training boils down to this simple notion and if you keep this in mind with each training initiative, you will be successful.

CHAPTER SIX
How to Socialize Your Cat

When it comes to training your cat to behave around other people, this can be a bit of a tricky situation. It can be embarrassing to have your cat hiss at guests or plop themselves right in the lap of the one person in the room who truly dislikes cats.

You might find yourself practically begging your cat to come and sit on your lap and he refuses time and time again. Let Aunt Margaret, the aunt who hates cats come over, and your cat is eager to jump right into her lap. So, what gives? Is your cat playing mind games with you and others?

To understand your cat's odd behavior, let's take a look again at how he would act in the wild. Have you ever watched your cat stalking its prey? Whether it be a mouse or cricket, your cat will respond the same. They watch from a distance and wait for the perfect moment and then they react and POUNCE!

If your cat has never been exposed to another cat, you may not know the following fact to be true. When two cats are "sizing one another up" they will stare at one another for what seems like ages. In a sense, the two cats are having a staring contest and they are going to decide the winner. The one who looks away first is considered the loser and the other the victor. With the following cat socialization tips, you can rest assured your cat will behave around others.

~Look him in the eye until he looks away~

As an exercise, sit down with your cat and stare at him, eye to eye. If he looks away before you do, you will know he considers you dominant over him. If you find yourself looking away first, he thinks he has won in the dominance category. Try it out from time to time to test how your cat is doing in regards to seeing you as the dominant one in the home. You might just be surprised at the results.

So, how does this relate to how your cat views humans? When there is a room full of people, it is inevitable the ones who like cats are going to be staring at the cat. They will think he is absolutely adorable and will fixate their eyes on him. The one who hates cats will rarely stare at a cat unless they are afraid and want to know where he is at all times.

Your cat is more likely to go to the one person who is not looking at him because he considers himself to be dominant over that person. According to your cat, this means he owns Aunt Margaret. Although it can be difficult training a cat to respond appropriately to company, there are some tips that can help.

The best time to start socializing a cat is when they are a kitten and have not developed a bad attitude or become skittish around strangers. If you are the only human in your home, plan on inviting family and friends over to get to know your new furry friend.

Exposing a kitten to different people and social situations at an early age will help them to overcome their shyness and discover how to properly act around other humans. If you have an older cat that is not behaving around others, distraction may be the key.

~Tips for getting your cat to leave guests alone~

Although it is difficult to believe, there are some people who simply do not like cats. For whatever reason, a cat is just not their cup of tea so it is important to teach your cat limits so they will know when it is okay to socialize and when it is best to stay back and observe.

If you find your cat is always drawn to that one person that seems to dislike them, you may find yourself putting your cat in a contained area until company leaves. Unfortunately, this can backfire and cause even more problems, eventually making your cat wary of any visitors.

Next time you have company, pay careful attention to how your cat responds. At what point does he seem to want to jump into the lap of Aunt Margaret? If you can discover what to look for, you can create a distraction that will prevent him from gaining access to her lap and causing a problem with your guest.

Have his favorite cat toy ready, such as a catnip-infused stuffed mouse, and toss it in the opposite direction of Aunt Margaret or any other cat hater. If it catches his eye at just the right moment, his attention will be diverted and he will spring for the toy instead of your guest.

If you do this each time he is ready to spring into action and cause you embarrassment, he may stop the behavior entirely. If this doesn't work, you can employ the help of the one who dislikes cats and have them stare eye to eye with your cat until the cat looks away. This will mean your guest has won dominance over the cat and the cat is likely to lose interest.

~Introducing your cat to children or babies~

It is important to note, a parent should never purchase or adopt a cat as a present for a young child. Although well-meaning parents do this all the time to teach their child responsibility, it can actually cause problems. Some cats simply do not like children and feel uncomfortable around them and rightly so. Small children like to pull a cat's tail or pick them up when they are not ready to be loved and can lead to the cat lashing out in fear and discomfort.

If a parent plans on getting a cat for a child, it is best to wait until the child is old enough to know how to properly care for the cat and how to handle them. It is a big responsibility caring for any pet and cats certainly are not an exception. Ideally, a parent should get a kitten for their child so the kitten can grow accustomed to the child before developing anti-social behaviors.

~Be cautious with cats and babies~

When introducing a cat to a baby, it is imperative the owner takes time in the process. Many people fear having a cat with a baby and for the most part, these fears are unfounded.

A cat will not steal the breath of your baby, no matter how many horror movies say he will. There is a danger in leaving cats and babies alone and it is not what most people think.

Cats love to snuggle with babies and will sometimes lay over the child's mouth, not meaning to hurt the baby, but just to snuggle close and show love. Unfortunately, this can cause a baby to inhale some of the cat's fur which can cause lung irritations and even upper respiratory infections. The cat can also lay over the child's nose and mouth, blocking them from being able to breathe. Never leave a cat unattended around a baby.

So, now that we have cleared up the reasons for actual fears, how can a cat owner introduce their cat to their new baby? Before we delve further into training, it is important to see things from your cat's perspective.

If your cat has never been exposed to babies or even children, they are likely to see your new baby as a screaming creature from Mars. Babies and children sound, look and especially smell different than adults. Unfortunately, these differences can cause a cat to go into a protective mode where they run and hide from this unknown creature or go into attack mode where they try to drive it away. Neither of these reactions is something a cat owner wants.

~Tips for preparing kitty before the baby arrives~

You have nine months to prepare your cat for the new baby and if you start early, there will be less of a learning curve for your cat and yourself. The following steps should be taken to ensure your cat will be ready to properly meet and socialize with your new bundle of joy.

- Obtain a recording of a newborn baby crying and play it from time to time so your cat grows accustomed to this strange sound. That way, he will not freak out when the real thing begins to occur.

  If the sound of the baby crying makes the cat curious to check it out, reward him with a special treat. If he grows upset hearing the baby crying, try to play with him, using a special toy before attempting to let him hear the cry again.

- Cats are curious creatures and they are going to want to check out all the new things you are buying for the baby. Allow the cat to explore and sniff but prevent him from sleeping on the items. One great way to keep a cat out of a baby's space is to use plastic rug protectors and place them nub side up. When placed at the door of the nursery or around the baby furniture, the cat is less likely to try to gain entrance.

- A couple of months before the baby arrives begin wearing baby powder and lotion. This will help your cat to grow accustomed to these new smells and associate them with you so the baby's smells will be familiar to him.

- Make schedule changes gradually, before the baby even arrives so your cat is not suddenly faced with getting less attention all at once. Subtle transitions are always preferable over sudden changes.

- Before introducing your cat to your baby, take an item of your baby's clothing and allow your cat to smell it and rub his scent on it. When you do this, it is a safe way of introducing your cat to your baby without risking any adverse reactions. With this method, it will not be such a shock when he actually meets the baby face to face.
- You can also try petting your cat with the baby's socks and then turn them inside out and put them on your baby, making sure the fur-covered side is out. When the cat smells himself on the socks, he is more likely to accept the baby as a member of the family.

Generally speaking, most cats are really good with babies. Your attitude will greatly dictate how the cat responds to the baby. Some new parents make a mistake by making a grand entrance and a big deal when bringing their baby home. This can create needless stress for the cat.

Instead, simply bring the baby in like he has been there all along. If the cat seems curious, allow him to sniff the baby without shooing him away. When the cat behaves appropriately, make sure you reward him so he associates a positive outcome.

Create opportunities that allow the cat to associate good things with the baby. When you are feeding the baby, try giving the cat a treat or tossing his favorite toy across the room. This will allow the cat to associate positive feelings when the baby is around.

As your baby grows older, it will be your responsibility to teach him to respect your cat. Do not allow the child to pull the cat's tail or corner the cat. If you create boundaries from the beginning, this will help to foster a positive relationship between your cat and child.

Although it can take time to properly socialize a cat and get them used to others, it can be done, even if a cat is older and has never been around others. The key to success is to proceed slowly and make sure the cat is fully comfortable with you before you go introducing strangers to the lineup.

If you proceed with caution, offer plenty of treats along the way, and work to make your cat comfortable around others, you will see positive changes in his behavior when you have company or take him out into the world to meet others.

CHAPTER SEVEN
How to Keep Your Cat Off the Counters

Talk to any cat owner and one of the first things you will hear them complain about is their cat wanting to climb up on their kitchen counters or even sit on their table. While some cat owners do not mind this, not everyone is thrilled to have a cat walking around on the surfaces they prepare food on.

Although it can seem like a constant battle to keep cats off counters, proper training can stop him from wanting to sit on your counters and table and it doesn't take long to make it happen. With this chapter's information, you will learn how to keep your cat off of any surface, including your kitchen counters, stove, and table. The sooner you implement these strategies into your training, the sooner these bad habits will be eliminated.

One of the most common reasons cats will jump up on a counter, stove, or table is for the reward of food. They do not understand you do not want their grimy paws prancing all around your food prep areas, they are just looking for the reward of food.

When you keep open food in these areas, your cat is bound to sniff them out and jump up to get a bite. This rewards him for his effort and makes him think this is an acceptable and rewarding experience. The first step in keeping your cat off your counters is making sure you make the experience unrewarding.

Your counters should be free of food and food residue at all times. Use a citrus-based cleaner to keep your counters clean of any spills and crumbs. As we discussed earlier in the book, cats hate the smell of citrus so this will be a safe deterrent to them.

In addition to keeping the counters, stove, and table free of any traces of food, you can also purchase cheap plastic placemats from the dollar store. Using two-sided tape, place the placemats on the counter and table, being sure to place them in the areas where your cat tends to jump up on. Make sure to place some of the tape on the top of the placemats as well.

Cats do not like sticky or uncomfortable surfaces. When he jumps up and feels a sensation he does not like with his paws, he is more likely to immediately jump down. It takes about a week for a cat to develop a new habit so give him time.

Instead of punishing him or running to pick him up each time he jumps on the counter, completely ignore him. Only react positively when he gets down. After about a week of using the placemats, you will begin to see your cat is jumping up less and less and will eventually lose complete interest.

Some cat owners find it helpful to play with their cat just before preparing a meal. Spend some one-on-one time with him and allow him to play with full energy. This will tire him out a bit and make him more willing to relax and take a nap while you are busy cooking and eating.

Because cats enjoy high places and being able to look down on the world around them, your kitchen cabinets and table provide tempting spots. To lessen the temptation, why not provide him with his own high place to sit on? Consider investing in a cat tower and offer him a treat each time he climbs up and sits on it. This may just make him less interested in your kitchen areas because he has his own and it offers rewards.

If the cat continues to jump on the counters and table, it will help for you to confine him to his own space while you are cooking and eating. Make sure the space has his litter box, food, and water. It should also contain a scratching post and toys so he enjoys his time spent there and does not feel as if he is being punished. This area is meant to provide a distraction to the cat so you can safely prepare and enjoy your food without having your cat cause disruptions and track germs.

Again, setting boundaries from a young age is much easier than attempting to overcome bad habits that have developed over weeks, months, and years. The more you work with your cat when he is young, the better the chances you will not face such a big challenge in training once he is older.

CHAPTER EIGHT
Training a Cat to Sleep In His Bed

Trying to make your cat sleep in his own bed at night can be difficult, especially if he has developed a habit of sleeping with you. Not every cat owner enjoys waking up to their cat sleeping on their head. If you find it difficult to share the bed with your cat, then this chapter is for you. Not only will you gain advice on finding the right cat bed, you will also be able to learn some helpful tips that will ensure your cat ends up sleeping there.

~Finding the right cat bed~

The first thing you will need to do is to purchase the right cat bed for your cat. As with any type of pet product, there are a wide variety of types and they simply boil down to your cat's preferences. The following steps will help to ensure you make the right purchase so your cat will have his very own cat bed and you can sleep comfortably all night without waking to a cat in your face.

- First, make sure you measure the length of your cat from head to tail. This is especially important, depending on how your cat sleeps. If your cat curls up to sleep, size may not matter as much but if he is one that likes to fully stretch out, you will need to make sure you purchase a bed that is long and wide enough to fit him.

- It is important you consider your cat when purchasing his cat bed. Cats that are older and suffer from joint problems will need thicker beds that offer more support. For cats who like to hide, a covered bed that looks like a soft igloo might be better. It is wise to research the different types and think about your cat's needs before you make a purchase. Some cats may find it comforting to sleep in a heated cat bed.

- It is a good idea to check out the material the cat bed is made of to make sure it is washable. Cat beds can become very dirty over time and they need to be washed on a regular basis to keep them free of germs and odors. If the cat bed is not machine washable, pass it up and find another one that is.

~Tips for getting started on training~

As you know by now, cats will not do something just because their owner wants them to. There has to be an incentive that draws them to sleep in the bed. Before you get started on training him to sleep in the cat bed, you will need to make sure you choose the perfect spot.

If your cat has been sleeping in your bedroom, you may want to first place the cat bed in your room. This will help make your cat feel more at ease as he transitions from sleeping in the bed with you to sleeping in his own bed. As he grows accustomed to sleeping in his cat bed, you can eventually move it to a more desirable location.

~Make his cat bed more attractive to him~

One of the first things you will need to do before you introduce your cat to his new cat bed is to make sure it doesn't smell like it just came from the factory. Cats have an extremely sensitive nose and do not enjoy strange or chemical smells.

To lure your cat into his cat bed, you will need to have some treats on hand as well as catnip. If your cat is accustomed to sleeping with you, it can help to place one of your old T-shirts on his bed so he feels close to you.

You can also try holding out a treat to your cat and luring him to the bed. If he follows you over to the bed, hold the treat over his head until he sits down. If he sits down inside his cat bed, make sure to reward him with a treat. Each time he sits or lies in his bed, reward him with a treat until he becomes comfortable sleeping in his bed.

Catnip is a great way to help a cat love his new bed. Rub catnip all over the new cat bed and place the bed wherever you plan on your cat sleeping. He should become very interested by the scent of the catnip and want to go check it out.

~Deter your cat from sleeping in other places~

If your cat still seems to prefer sleeping in the laundry basket instead of his new cat bed, it is important to make this and other prime sleeping spots no longer attractive to him. Luckily, there are some natural deterrents you can use to harmlessly deter your cat from taking a nap in unwanted areas.

- Cover your laundry basket or other sleep spots with aluminum foil. Cats dislike the feel of this material and will likely avoid the area.
- You can also spray a strong citrus spray on your laundry basket, bed, or other favorite cat sleeping spots so he is more likely to choose his cat bed.

If you consistently work with your cat, you will soon find he loves his cat bed and will want to take naps in it all the time. It is important to keep the cat bed in a consistent place until he grows accustomed to sleeping there. Once he has fully embraced his new sleeping space, you can move the cat bed to a more desirable location.

~Quick tips for making sure your cat loves his cat bed~

- Place the cat bed by a window. Cats love a bed with a view and this will likely encourage your cat to sit on the bed and eventually drift off into a peaceful sleep as he watches the birds fly by.
- Elevate the cat bed so it is off the ground. Cats love being perched high above and will be more likely to investigate a cat bed if it rests in a

position that allows them to look down on the world around them.

- If your cat absolutely refuses to stop sleeping on your couch or chair, you can try placing the cat bed on top. Although it might seem a bit counterproductive, this can at least prevent him from shedding all over your furniture.
- If your cat seems to totally ignore the cat bed, keep moving it until you find a spot that interests him. This might require a period of trial and error but you will eventually find the ideal spot.

If at first, he does not seem too keen on trying out his new cat bed, do not give up. As with any training, it takes a bit of coaxing and rewarding to get a cat interested in what you are trying to teach him.

CHAPTER NINE
How to Clicker Train Your Cat

By reading this book, you have learned many different methods of cat training that revolve around association. This book would not be fully complete without helping you gain an understanding of how to clicker train cat. Although it might seem a little intimidating, the process is not any more difficult than the other means of training. You simply need to understand how to clicker train your cat and why it works.

~The science behind clicker training your cat~

Before we get into the actual details of training your cat with a clicker, it is important you understand how clicker training works. Click training is considered a form of operant conditioning with the clicker being the stimulus that helps the cat connect the treat with the action they just performed.

It was originally developed by BF Skinner to help train pigeons but can be used for cats, dogs, and even other animals. The clicker tool is used to make a distinct sound but cat owners sometimes whistle or make clicking sounds with their mouth. The result is the same as long as your cat hears the sound and responds.

When an owner is attempting to train their cat with a new behavior, the owner clicks the clicker at the precise moment their cat does the desired behavior and then a treat is offered. There are a few steps involved in this training but all it takes is time and effort.

~Information for skeptical cat owners~

When cat owners first discover the steps to clicker train cat, they often think the process cannot possibly work. It seems strange a simple clicking sound could help train a cat but there is scientific evidence to back up this sort of training.

If you think about it, your cat has already been trained with operant conditioning using a sound. If you do not believe it, get out your electric can opener and start opening a can. If you have ever fed your cat canned tuna, he is likely going to come running just because he hears the sound of the can opener. He associates the sound of the can opener with the reward of tuna. All you need to do now is make him associate the clicking noise with a treat and you are on your way to training.

~Easy steps to training your cat with a clicker~

The first thing you will need to do is to purchase your cat clicker. They are available from many retailers online and can be purchased in pet supply stores. Some people prefer to use the click of a ballpoint pen and others prefer making a sound with their mouth. It is up to you which method you use for clicking. You may find your cat prefers one method over another.

Just like with other means of training, you need to make sure you choose a cat treat that is truly enticing to your cat. If it is a treat he receives all the time, why would he bother making an extra effort to get it?

It is important to choose a cat treat that is pungent because cats use their sense of smell first and then their taste. Some cats will prefer a fishy aroma while others may prefer a smoked turkey smell and taste.

You will not need to give your cat a large amount for each reward. A small piece, no bigger than the end of your finger, is plenty to give as a reward. Giving too much may disrupt his nutrition and this is something you do not want.

To get started on training, you will need to help your cat associate the sound of the click with his treat. When you teach him this, he will learn every time he hears the click, something good is about to happen.

To do this, simply sit down with your cat and the treats. Have your clicker ready. You will click the clicker, toss him a treat, click the clicker, and toss him a treat. Do this several times to allow your cat to begin to learn.

Remember: cats will not train as long as dogs will so short training sessions are preferable over longer ones. You also do not want to train with him so long that he becomes full and can no longer hold any more treats because this can be counterproductive.

Before long, you will begin to notice your cat looks towards the treat bag each time you click the clicker. This means you have gotten his attention and he now associates that sound with a delicious treat.

~Start catching him in the act~

Perhaps you want to clicker train your cat to sleep in his cat bed or to scratch on his scratching post. All you need to do is sit around and wait for your cat to do that behavior you want him to do.

The minute he sits on his cat bed or scratches on his post, you will make the clicking sound and then immediately give him his treat. He might look at you a little puzzled at first but he will soon realize he is doing something to make the click and get the treat.

To ensure your cat is properly trained with the clicker method, it is imperative you click at the precise moment. If you are training for sitting and your cat suddenly stands and you click when he stands, he will not be able to associate the click with sitting.

If your cat responds well to clicker training, you can use this method for training him to accept his new cat bed, walk with a harness, or even sit. While this method of training is not for every cat owner, it can certainly help those who are finding other methods to be difficult.

CHAPTER TEN
Harness Training Your Cat

While some cat owners would think walking a cat on a leash to be absurd, there are actually practical reasons for training a cat to walk on a leash. Cats love going outdoors but it is not always safe to let them run wild. Training a cat to walk with a harness allows you and your cat to enjoy the great outdoors without the risk. This also allows you to develop a deeper bond with your cat.

~Leashes aren't just for dogs anymore~

Now that the "cat" is outta the bag, so to speak, it is clear cats can be trained to walk with a leash and actually enjoy it. To be clear, not every cat is going to want to walk on a leash but why not give your cat the opportunity to see if he does?

Walking your cat on a leash allows him to receive valuable exercise so his joints stay strong and healthy and he avoids tipping the scales, which can put his health at risk. This cat harness and leash training can sometimes help timid cats gain confidence in exploring the world around them.

~How to purchase the best cat harness~

If you plan on training your cat to walk on a leash, it is wise you purchase a cat harness instead of using a collar. If you walk a cat with a traditional collar, your cat can sometimes slip out of the collar and escape, putting his life in danger.

The first thing you will need to do before you purchase the best cat harness is to measure your cat's chest with a flexible measuring tape. This will measure your cat's girth so you will know what size of harness to purchase.

When you are first attempting to train your cat with a harness, you may want to consider a vest harness because these are more comfortable than some types. These also equally distribute the pressure placed on the cat's frame so there is no irritation.

It is important to choose a cat harness that fits snugly but is not too tight. The harness should fit securely at the neck, girth, and belly. To test how well the cat harness fits, slide one finger between the harness and your cat. If you can fit more than one finger, the harness is too loose and will need to be adjusted or a different size purchased.

~Help your cat grow accustomed to the harness~

Training a cat to wear a harness might seem like a daunting task but like all cat training, it simply takes time and dedication. One of the first tips for how to put a harness on a cat is to bring the harness home and leave it lying around where your cat can smell it, mark it with their scent glands, and play with it. Training should not be attempted until the cat feels comfortable being around the harness and it smells like home.

You should work on harness training your cat indoors before ever venturing outside with him. Properly place your cat in the harness and let him walk around with it on. At first, he may flop over and act weird but do not let this alarm you. He will soon realize the harness is nothing to fear. When he walks around with the harness on, make sure you give him a treat as a reward.

It can also be helpful to attach the cat leash and allow him to drag it around the house and play with it. Doing this for a few days will help your cat to fear the harness and leash less and even grow used to wearing them. This is important for ensuring he will eventually allow you to walk him on the leash.

When you decide your cat is ready to walk on the leash outside, it is best if you try things out in an enclosed area that does not have a lot of stimuli that might cause distractions with your cat.

Walk around, leading him with the leash and allow him to sniff around outside and grow comfortable being led on the leash. Some cat owners find it helpful to drive to a remote area, away from other people and animals, to train their cat to walk with a harness and leash.

Word of caution: Once your cat gets a taste for the outdoors, they may develop a bad habit of wanting to run out the door each time it is opened. You will need to work with your cat and let him know the only time he can go outside is when he is wearing his harness and is on a leash.

Although it might seem a little intimidating harness training a cat, the process is not that tough as long as you follow the above steps and offer rewards along the way. If you train for a few weeks and your cat simply will not walk on a leash, he may just be a cat that does not enjoy walking with a harness.

CHAPTER ELEVEN
Can You Really Teach a Cat Tricks...Like a Dog?

Now that you have a better grasp on why your cat exhibits certain behaviors and how you can curb unwanted ones, it is time to have a little fun. You got a cat so you would have a companion, right? This portion of the training guide is fully for you and your cat to bond together and have fun while training.

Before you even begin to question cats being trained to do tricks, you need to know, it is not going to be easy. If you have had some success with the other methods of training, you will find training your cat to do tricks isn't any more difficult.

As we have discussed time and time again, cats are all about rewards. If the reward is not there, the cat tricks will not be performed. When you attempt to train your cat to do a few tricks, just remember, you must ALWAYS have a reward to offer, even after your cat has mastered the trick and seems to perform it without a fuss. If you suddenly stop offering his reward, you will likely find the tricks stop too.

Just like training a dog, you need to make sure you only work on one trick at a time. Trying to introduce too many tricks at once will only lead to confusion on the part of your cat and irritation on your part. Start with the easiest of tricks and then work your way up, allowing your cat time to master each one before moving on to the next.

~Basic tricks you can teach your cat~

There are four basic cat tricks we will cover in this chapter. Once you have learned the techniques and become comfortable with training your cat, you may think of other ones you can introduce along the way. Just make sure you refresh your cat's memory on a regular basis so he does not forget his training. Always offer a reward with each successful trick performed.

Teach him to come to you when you call him – This might seem like a no-brainer if you have ever owned a dog but you must remember, cats are completely different. Your cat could care less if you call him unless you have a can of tuna to offer or some other delectable treat.

When you call them, cats will often take a message and plan on getting back to you when and if they have time. With a little time and some treats, you can be successful at teaching your cat to come to you when you call him, even if he is busy grooming himself or taking a nap. When training your cat for this trick, make sure you choose a command word to use in addition to his name. Each time you call him with this command, such as "Fluffy, come!" you will offer him a treat if he does.

Do not make the mistake of only using his name with this trick command or he will end up expecting a treat each and every time he hears his name. Each time you use the command, he will begin associating this word with a treat and should come to you to get it. Do not reward him unless he does come to you when using the command word.

Teach him to stand on his hind legs – This trick might seem a little complicated but it is actually fairly easy, as long as you have a treat ready. All you will need to do is to hold his favorite treat over his head. When he sees the treat, he should become quite interested and stretch up on his hind legs in an attempt to reach the treat.

To ensure this works, you will need to state a command word each time you want him to practice the trick. You can use words like "up", "stand", or "sit up" but just make sure you use the same word each time.

You will only reward him with the treat when he will perform the trick without trying to get the treat out of your hand. Each time he tries to grab the treat, just ignore him and wait and try again. When he successfully rises without the reach, offer him the treat as a reward. Eventually, he will learn exactly what he needs to do to get his little treat as a reward.

Teach him to shake your hand – Shaking hands might seem like a trick only a dog would do but you can actually teach your cat to shake hands as well. It is best to start this trick when your cat is relaxed and is in a sitting position. You will need to reach out and touch your cat's paw and as a natural reaction, he will likely lift his paw. When he does this, hold his paw gently in your hand and give him a treat.

When you train him for this trick, make sure you use a command word so he will learn to associate the trick with that word. It is important you give a command word each time so he doesn't think he will get a treat each and every time you accidentally touch his paw.

As you continue doing this with him, he will eventually learn to give you his paw without you touching it. Make sure you reward him with a treat each time and he will oblige you by giving his paw and shaking hands.

Teach your cat to wave – Never seen a cat waving? If not, you are about to. This is an easy trick to teach your cat and is a fun one to show off to guests. All you will need to do is wave a treat back and forth in front of your cat. He will naturally move his paw back and forth in an attempt to swipe the treat and grab it for himself.

To ensure your cat understands you are teaching him a trick, make sure you use a command word when you do this. After he has made the waving motion with his paw, you will give him a treat. Once your cat seems to have the hang of this trick, do not let go of the treat until he begins to do it without trying to grab for the treat you are holding. Once he does the waving motion without going for the treat, make sure you reward him.

~Training for tricks is not the same as training against bad behavior~

It is important you realize training your cat to do a trick is entirely different than training him to stop his bad behavior. When it comes to training a cat to act appropriately, you are actually offering him alternatives to the "bad behavior" instead of training him to do anything. During behavior training, the cat is not actually learning anything. He is simply being given alternative methods of performing his natural instincts.

When it comes to teaching your cat tricks, he will actually learn. Although the training is different, association is still vital. When you are training your cat to do tricks, he will learn to associate receiving a treat with the trick and then the command with the trick. Eventually, he will come to realize when he hears the command and performs the trick he is able to receive the treat.

As we have discussed before, the goal of a cat is not to please you. Remember, he is not a dog. You must give him a treat each and every time he performs the trick. If you rarely give him the treat he is looking for, you are going to find he rarely does the trick. Consistency cannot be expected without consistency on your part, in offering him the expected treats for his hard work.

If you had wanted a pet that is consistently loyal and does everything you ask of him, you would have likely gotten a dog. People own cats because they like that cats have a mind of their own. They like the spunkiness of cats and do not want a lapdog. So, don't ever expect your cat to start acting like a dog, but do expect your cat can do many of the things your dog does, only in their own way.

CHAPTER TWELVE
Punishment vs Rewards

One of the most ineffective ways of attempting to train a cat is punishment. Physical punishment should never be given, regardless of what a cat does. When you swat at a cat or otherwise use some type of physical punishment, you are only teaching your cat to fear you and that is something you do not want to happen. It will actually cause him to act out more than he already does.

If you try to punish a cat, your actions are going to backfire. Anyone who has ever found a surprise in their shoe or on their bed likely knows how cats feel about their feeble attempts at punishment.

~Control your anger when dealing with your cat~

Some cat owners become overly frustrated with their cat and this leads to abuse. As a cat owner, you should never resort to physical punishments of any type because this is cruel to your cat and doesn't work at all. The following are some of the types of punishment cat owners should avoid if they want to foster a good relationship with their cat.

- No yelling
- No hitting
- No spanking
- No locking him in a room
- No withholding food
- No rubbing his nose in it
- No hitting him with any object
- No throwing objects at him

If you cannot deal with training your cat without resorting to the above behaviors, it is wise you find a new home for your cat and work on your aggression before bringing any pets into your home. A cat deserves an owner who will love and take care of them, not abuse and hurt them.

Violent actions will only cause truly bad behavior to be exhibited by your cat. He won't just do those things he has been doing that drive you nuts, he may end up attacking you or others as he lashes out over his treatment.

There is actually no way to punish a cat. If you spray him with a cat water bottle or make a loud sound, he is going to associate that action with you only. It will never stop him from doing something you do not want him doing. This is why so many cat owners erroneously think cats cannot be trained. The reason their cat seems to be untrainable is because the owner is attempting to use a system of punishment instead of rewards and this will simply never work.

You need to remember, in order to make your cat stop doing something, you need to make the action or item look much less attractive to your cat so he loses interest. You must also offer an alternative so he does not feel deprived of being a normal cat.

~Choose the right treats for your cat~

The rewards for performing a cat trick he has learned should always be an edible treat. There is a wide array of cat treats on the market and you may want to speak with your veterinarian to get some advice on healthy options so you are nourishing your cat while giving him a treat. Cats can sometimes be finicky so you may need to purchase a few different types of treats until you find the one he truly adores and will work for.

When considering training for behavioral issues, there really is no reward to be offered. You, as the owner, simply offer an alternative for your cat and he happily goes along, never realizing he has been "trained" to stop doing something.

~What if your cat starts truly acting out?~

If you suddenly find your cat is truly acting out and behaving in ways that have you wanting to pull your hair out, you must stand back and take a look at the situation. Cats are creatures of habit and prefer set schedules. They typically do not like chaotic or loud situations and they certainly hate change.

One of the number one causes of a cat acting out suddenly is stress. There are many things that can bring on stress for a cat so it is important to think about any changes to routine that may have caused the changes in behavior. The following are the most common stressors for cats.

- Moving to a new home
- Introducing new people to the family
- New pets in the home
- Change to his daily routine
- Isolation
- Confinement
- Death of a family member

- Family member on vacation
- Boredom and loneliness

If your cat is dealing with any of the above scenarios, it stands to reason this is why he is acting out. Instead of punishing your cat for acting out in a way you don't like, why not seek to fix the situation that is causing him to be stressed? This will help to protect the emotional and physical health of your cat and will help to stop any unwanted behaviors he suddenly starts to exhibit simply because he cannot cope with the stress.

~Try to get rid of the stress~

Unfortunately, you can't always eliminate the stress in your cat's life, just like you can't totally get rid of yours. The key to helping your cat is attempting to find the sources of stress you can eliminate or relieve and doing all you can to help your cat cope.

For those things you can't help, attempt to offer your cat plenty of affection and understanding as he goes through the process of growing accustomed to changes in your home and lifestyle. With reassurance and care, your cat will grow accustomed to the new situation and his odd behaviors will stop, just give him time to adjust.

CONCLUSION

The act of training a cat is not an overnight process but with time and effort, it can be accomplished. You will find the information and tips included in this book to help you better understand why your cat acts the way he does. If you are diligent and willing, you will begin to see your cat transform as he slowly changes his behavior.

Remember you are in control and your actions and attitude will very much decide how your cat responds to his training. Refer to this guide often, as you go through each stage of training. You may find you need to reread sections from time to time to fully understand the cat training techniques of working with positive association

No matter how rough the cat training seems at first, make sure you do not give up. Any cat can be trained; some just take longer than others.

Thank you for buying this book. If you would take a minute to write a review, I would very much appreciate it. It really helps me with sales and promotion.

Respectfully,
Butch Spillman

About the Author
Butch Spillman

Butch Spillman is an author with a heart for people. Born in Hollywood, California in 1946, Butch always seemed to have a dream that kept him going, even when leaving home at the tender age of 14, because he had no other choice. Life wasn't easy but Butch refused to ever give up, no matter how tough the road became.

Butch's vast career first involved him becoming a radio DJ, working the graveyard shift to pay the bills and enjoy the life experience it brought him. He would go on to work in many cities, lighting up the airways with his intoxicating personality, filled with humor and understanding.

At the age of eighteen, Butch Spillman set out on a journey to work in real estate and even acquired a General Contractor's license so he could begin building houses. He enjoyed the challenge the real estate industry brought to his life and he experienced great success in his endeavors.

Throughout his career, Butch has never stopped learning. Life taught him from an early age that he had to do for himself and keep working diligently to be successful and that is just what he did. No challenge was too great and he never accepted failures, constantly striving to better himself in all he chose to pursue.

Today, Butch is retired and although he has slowed down, he certainly has not stopped. Married to a beautiful wife, he has two grown sons and four grandchildren he loves immensely. Throughout his life,

Butch has always felt God's leading hand, guiding him on each path he has sought.

In the latest adventure of his life, Butch has set out to fulfill his lifelong dream of becoming a published author. With his skills and life knowledge, he seeks to educate, enlighten, entertain, and encourage readers of all ages.

Other Kindle eBooks and Paperbacks
by Butch Spillman

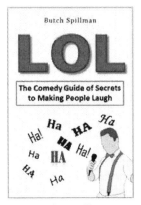

"LOL"

Comedy can be Learned.
This Guide teaches why people laugh,
how to do stand-up, write jokes and routines,
handle hecklers, market yourself, and more.

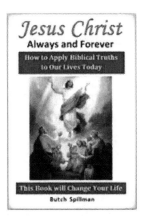

Jesus Christ, Always and Forever
How to Apply Biblical Truths
to Our Lives Today

How to Attract Butterflies

This little book shows you how fun and easy
it is to make your yard Butterfly Friendly. Learn
how to get their attention with bright colored plants, sunny areas, wind
protection, butterfly spas, and more...

52 Bedtime Stories

Children's Read-Aloud Short Stories,
each with a Moral Christian Lesson

1100 Fish Recipes

130 Salmon Recipes, 67 Cod Recipes, 50 Trout Recipes,
80 Halibut Recipes, 13 Red Snapper Recipes
plus over 650 more Recipes for 33 other Fish types.
Bonus Recipes include 100 Sauce Recipes,
14 Court Bouillon (Poaching Broth) Recipes,
100 Miscellaneous Fish Recipes and
27 Ways to Cook Frog Legs.

67 Quick & Easy Italian Meals

Great Italian Recipes and Menu Ideas

23705054R00059

Made in the USA
Lexington, KY
16 December 2018